The railway is affectionately known as 'The Poppy Line' thanks to Clement Scott, a journalist and poet who visited the area in Victorian times and christened it 'Poppyland'. Through his column in the Daily Telegraph, 'Poppyland' became a most fashionable area to visit, putting North Norfolk on the travellers' map.
To quote from the 'Garden of Sleep':

"Neath the blue of the sky in the green of the corn,
It is there that the royal red poppies are born!
Brief days of desire, and long dreams of delight,
They are mine when my Poppy-land cometh in sight."

The Poppy Line

Background: With ripening corn fields all around, NER J27 No. 65894 climbs the poppy-lined 1 in 80 incline towards Weybourne with the sea in the background in July 1997. Photo. Steve Allen

This railway is part of the former Melton Constable to Cromer Beach branch line, our section between Holt, Weybourne and Sheringham, along with the section to Cromer was built by the Eastern and Midlands Railway and opened on 16th June, 1887. Unlike most other railways of the time it was built to exploit the rapidly growing tourist market rather than to serve the local communities. Initially the line was intended to go from Holt to Blakeney to serve the harbour there, but when the directors realised the potential revenue from tourists visiting Clement Scott's 'Poppyland' they diverted the line along the coast to Cromer, leaving Blakeney harbour in splendid isolation to this day.

On 1st July 1893, the Eastern and Midlands Railway was amalgamated with other railways in East Anglia to form the Midland and Great Northern Joint Railway - known to many as the 'Joint' or more cynically as the 'muddle and go nowhere'.

The M&GN totalled some 160 miles in length, at its centre was Melton Constable which had grown as a railway town from a small village in deepest rural Norfolk. There were lines radiating from here to Cromer, Yarmouth and Lowestoft, Norwich and to King's Lynn where the line continued west to Peterborough with a branch to Spalding and Bourne, where connections could be made with the rest of the railway network.

The railway's works were situated at Melton Constable where its mainly second-hand locomotives, carriages and wagons were repaired, modified and even rebuilt. The

Company also built houses and a school for its workers, together with other facilities such as gas works, water storage tower, sewerage works, recreation ground and a bowling green. At Briston, the next village, a mission hall was built to keep some workers away from the demon drink! The Joint was unique in that for the majority of its length it was single line with passing loops, usually at the stations.

In 1923 when the other major railways of Britain were grouped to form the LNER (London &

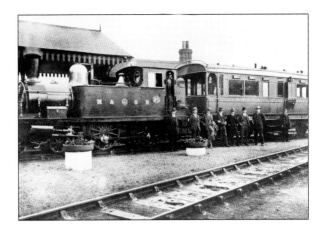

An M&GN 4-4-0T stands at Melton Constable station with inspection saloon.

North Eastern Railway), LMS (London Midland & Scottish), GWR (Great Western Railway) and SR (Southern Railway) the M&GN unusually remained an independent company under joint control of the LMS and the LNER. In 1936 the LNER took over full ownership of the M&GN. They did little to develop the M&GN, as they already owned the old Great Eastern Railway, which served many of the places also served by the Joint.

M&GN locomotives undergoing repairs inside Melton Constable Works.

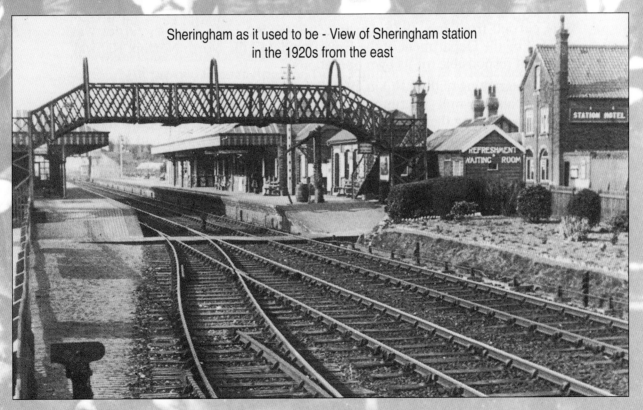

Sheringham as it used to be - View of Sheringham station in the 1920s from the east

When the railways were nationalised in 1948 the former M&GN lines became part of British Railways. With changing holiday and transport patterns, revenue from the line declined throughout the 1950s leading to almost total closure on 28th February, 1959. One of the few surviving sections, Cromer to Melton Constable, stayed open until 1964 when the line was closed between Melton Constable and Sheringham. The remaining section from Sheringham to Cromer is still part of the Railtrack national network, with a passenger service using modern diesel Sprinter units run by Anglia Railways.

As soon as the M&GN closure notices were posted in early 1959, others pleading 'Save the M&GN by joining the M&GN Joint Railway Preservation Society' were put up. The early preservation schemes were to say the least unrealistic, with enthusiasm and idealism over-riding common sense. The schemes included the preservation and operation of: -

a) All 163 miles of the former M&GN.
b) The 22 miles from North Walsham to Great Yarmouth.
c) The line from North Walsham to Aylsham.
d) The line from Melton Constable to Norwich City Station.
e) The line from Melton Constable to Hindolvestone.

A quiet corner of Sheringham station

The Society was busying itself raising funds. A popular way of doing this was to run 'last trip' railtours over the already closed branches of the M&GN and GER before the track was lifted. By 1964 the aims of the Society had become more realistic and when the section from Melton Constable to Sheringham closed they had raised sufficient funds to purchase the 3-mile section from Weybourne to Sheringham. Initially, the Society founded its headquarters at Weybourne station. By the time the paperwork had been completed, demolition contractors had already removed all of the track and sidings at Weybourne.

British Rail continued to use Sheringham station until 1967 when they built a halt on the Cromer side of the level crossing on Station Road. The Society then took a lease on the station and transferred its activities there. The first of the Society's rolling stock - two locomotives (B12/3 4-6-0 no. 61572, and J15 0-6-0 no. 65462), two modern Diesel Railbuses and the 'Quadart' coaches - arrived on 4th June 1967.

The Society was not legally permitted to operate a railway as it was not a limited company. Therefore a private company, Central Norfolk Enterprises Limited, had been formed for this purpose. In 1969 the name was changed to the North Norfolk Railway Company and went public to raise capital by offering shares, initially raising £14,000.

Two Light Railway Orders were needed to allow the Company to carry fare-paying passengers. Initially, only members of the M&GNJRS could be carried and day membership was available at the ticket office. After a public enquiry the first Light Railway Order was granted to British Rail acting on behalf of the Company, this meant that after detailed inspection by BR of engines, passenger

LNER B12 4-6-0 No. 8572 in a 1930s cameo scene at Weybourne.

Since taking possession in 1965 the volunteers had re-laid the track through Weybourne station ready for the time when it would be possible to run trains again. The railway continued acquiring further locomotives and rolling stock for use on the line, including two historic directors' saloons and two former Brighton Belle Pullman cars.

stock and operating personnel, members of the public were carried from July 1975.

In 1976 the second Light Railway Order was granted by the Department of the Environment to the North Norfolk Railway making it responsible for its own operations.

GER J15 0-6-0 No. 564 runs around its train at Weybourne in July 1988. Photo. Steve Allen

Since the granting of the LRO in 1976 the railway has expanded and achieved many goals. The most notable achievement being the rebuilding of the derelict railway to the new station at Holt. The rails had been removed in 1967 and the track bed had in places become overgrown with some saplings over four inches in diameter. Between 1980 and 1989 when it re-opened to steam trains, volunteers toiled every weekend to clear the undergrowth and relay the track, also building a platform at the site of the new Holt station.

The Society's J15 locomotive was completely overhauled and returned to traffic in 1977; followed in 1978 by the stalwart Hunslet saddletank Ring Haw which has steamed every season since! Due to the difficulty of restoring these locos in the open, the railway purchased the engine shed from Norwich City station and re-erected it at Weybourne in 1980 to provide covered workshop accommodation. This was extended in 1990 by the addition of a period style machine shop.

The Society's prestigious LNER B12/3 locomotive No. 8572 was returned to steam in 1995 after more than 30 years out of use. This followed a protracted restoration project that culminated in its rebuilding at a steam loco works in former East Germany.

For operational reasons the railway has accumulated a number of diesels. The two diesel railbuses have now been on the NNR three times longer than they spent on BR and are still doing sterling work on off-peak trains. These have more

The railway's Class 117 Diesel Multiple Unit

BR Class 37 Co-Co locomotive No. D6732 'Mirage' at Weybourne station in June 1997. Photo. Steve Allen

recently been augmented by the arrival on the NNR of a former BR Class 117 DMU set. A number of shunters (industrial and ex-BR) are used on works trains and on shunting duties. One of the restrictions of running over the heathland to Holt is that during times of 'high fire risk' specified by the fire brigade, the railway is not allowed to use steam engines between Weybourne and Holt. Because of this the NNR has a number of mainline diesel locomotives which can haul the trains should the need arise. These include Class 27 D5386 (ex-27 066), Class 25 D5207 (ex-25 057) and Class 37 D6732 (ex-37 032).

Restored BR Mk1 TSO coach M4843.
This type of coach forms the backbone of the NNR's operational fleet. Photo.Steve Allen

The railway has continued to increase its rolling stock from the first arrivals in 1967. Most of these have been BR Mark 1 coaches which now form

the mainstay of the passenger services, one of these being No. E3868 which was built at York in 1953 and was the first preserved Mark 1 coach, being purchased by the NNR in 1968. It has now worked far longer on the NNR than it did on BR!

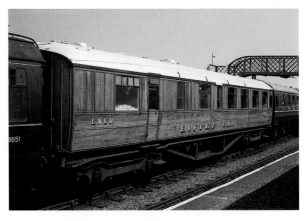

LNER Gresley Buffet car No. 51769.
Photo. Steve Allen

Among the wooden-bodied coaches on the NNR is the Society's superb award winning 1937 LNER Gresley Buffet Car 51769 whose restoration started in the sidings at Norwich Victoria station in 1977 and was completed after ten long years in 1987 at Sheringham. This coach is often used in service trains to provide drinks and light refreshments. Another of the Society's coaches, the Gresley TK (third corridor) 3395, has been cosmetically restored.

One of the most popular aspects of preserved railways, with the NNR being no exception, is the chance to enjoy a meal whilst travelling leisurely through the countryside behind a steam engine. To this end the NNR decided in 1990 to refurbish the two former Brighton Belle Pullman cars as a dedicated dining set. They also converted a former BG (brake guards) Mark 1 coach to be a kitchen car. During the running season this train serves Sunday lunches, and evening meals on selected Friday and Saturday evenings.

With all this rolling stock to be accommodated many sidings have been laid at Sheringham, Weybourne and Holt. The main line is also undergoing gradual replacement mainly with the longer lasting concrete sleepers. Signalling too has come on a long way since 1976 when there was only one operational signal on the railway. In 1980, Wensum Junction signal box was relocated from Norwich to the site of the former Sheringham West box. This was demolished by BR in 1965 to prevent vandalism! The lever frame in the Wensum Junction box came from Loughton on the London Underground Central Line (previously the GER) and was the last used mechanical signal box on the Underground. The signal box at Weybourne was relocated from Holt in 1967; it was recommissioned in 1989 following a lengthy overhaul allowing the railway to run a more intensive service for passengers.

Inside of Weybourne signalbox

GNR N2 0-6-2T No. 69523 runs past the former Wensum Junction signalbox now at Sheringham in August 1994. Photo. Steve Allen

There is a place for civil engineering on the NNR too. The responsibility for the bridges passed to the railway with the LRO in 1976. Bridge 303 over the main A149 coast road was in poor condition and had to be replaced if the railway was to continue to run. In 1982, BR culverted a ditch in the fens, making a bridge surplus to their requirements, this was bought by the NNR for reuse as bridge 303. Masterminded by NNR volunteers and BR bridge engineer David Pinkerton, it was replaced in the Autumn of 1984. Before the extension to Holt could be started bridge 301 over Spring Beck near Weybourne station had to have its brick arch waterproofed. This entailed removing several tons of infill, so that the exposed arch could be painted with bitumen sealant. A footbridge had to be erected at Weybourne to enable the NNR to run a two train service. The Stowmarket footbridge was being replaced due to electrification of the main London to Norwich line and it was purchased from BR. In 1989 it was re-erected by volunteers at Weybourne using the railway's steam crane.

Hunslet Austerity 0-6-0ST No. 3809 crosses the A149 on bridge 303 in February 1994. This bridge was replaced by volunteers in 1984. Photo. Debbie Allen

Background: Great Northern Railway N2 0-6-2T No. 69523 runs past the harvested corn fields near Sheringham Golf Course in August 1994. Photo. Steve Allen

"WE'LL MEET AGAIN"

*RELIVING THOSE
GOOD OLD-BAD OLD DAYS
OF THE 1940s - RATIONING,
CHILDREN'S EVACUATION
AND FOND FAREWELLS.*

Occasionally the NNR arranges themed weekends,
these evocative pictures were taken
during a 1940s event. Photos. Brian Chambers

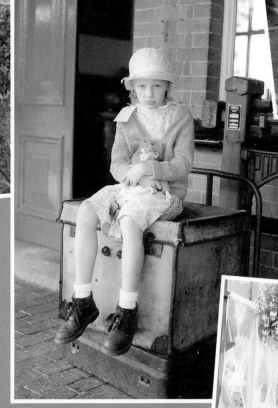

Wright's
COAL TAR
Soap

REFRESHES
AFTER TRAVEL

Stephens
For ALL
Fountain Pens
Inks

Exploring the Railway

When the station was built in 1887 it stood in open countryside and Sheringham was a small fishing village. With the arrival of the railway, tourism soon took off and many houses were built around the station although original flint cottages are still to be seen at the seaward end of the town. There is still a small fleet of boats based here which go fishing for lobsters and crabs. These boats can be seen drawn up the gently sloping beach when not in use. The station started off as a typical M&GN 'hall and cross wings' building and grew with the town that it served until it became what you see today.

The entrance to Sheringham station for those not arriving by train is through the original booking hall. Tickets should be purchased here. Walking onto the platform you will find the souvenir shop and station buffet to your right. This is also the main platform for train departures. To the left at the end of the main station building, you may note a small red brick building currently used as an office. The origins of this building date back to the inter-company rivalry between the M&GN and GER when back in 1906 the GER were finally able to run their trains to Sheringham from Cromer. Because the M&GN did not wish the GER to take over their facilities they built a room specifically for GER staff. This room is still affectionately known as the GE room. Opposite this a small wooden footbridge leads across to platform two. On either side of the footbridge you will find non-

operational locomotives on display. One of these is likely to be the fireless locomotive, which could carry out short periods of shunting in factory sidings after taking steam under pressure from the factory boiler house. This was especially useful in high fire risk areas, this loco was employed at Procter and Gamble's West Thurrock chemical works in Essex. Another loco you may also see here is a small tank engine called Wissington. This engine was donated to the Society in 1977 by the British Sugar Corporation having spent its working life on the Wissington Railway in the Fens near Downham Market.

On operational days, platform two is normally used for some train departures and for engines to 'run round' their train. The WH.Smith bookstall is on long-term loan from the National Railway Museum, having stood for many years on the concourse of London's Waterloo Station. This is now used as a model railway shop and is

GER J15 0-6-0 No. 564 runs around its train at Sheringham station. Photo. Steve Allen

SHERINGHAM
'TWIXT SEA AND PINE

Interior of Sheringham Station Buffet

points in that area, as well as the level crossing gates. You are welcome to pull the levers but please mind your fingers!

The remainder of platform three is used to store the East Coast Pullman dining train when not in use.

open most days. There once were buildings comprising offices and waiting rooms here on platform two with a glazed canopy that matched the one on platform one and it is the railway's intention to rebuild this at some time in the future if at all possible.

Beyond the bookstall on platform three are the Society's museum coaches. These comprise an old LNER parcels van built in 1945 to an austere design to last only ten years, and an LNER Gresley TK. The history of the M&GN and the NNR is displayed here in old photographs and artefacts.

The signal box, which comes next, is open for viewing. This is now a non-operational signal box, which for many years was situated alongside the level crossing on Station Road. There, as Sheringham East box, it controlled signals and

BUFFET & REFRESHMENTS

Flagship of the North Norfolk Railway's fleet -
The M&GN Society's award winning LNER B12
4-6-0 No. 8572 climbs the 1 in 80 gradient
towards Weybourne station in April 1996.
Photo. Steve Allen

SHERINGHAM TO WEYBOURNE

This stretch of line passes through a designated scenic Area of Outstanding Natural Beauty, where development of any kind is strictly controlled.

LMS 8F 2-8-0 No. 48305 departs from Sheringham under bridge 305. Photo. Steve Allen

A distant view showing that it certainly isn't flat in this part of Norfolk! Skelding Hill dominates as Ring Haw runs past Sheringham Golf Course in August 1992. Photo. Debbie Allen

GNR 0-6-0ST No. 1247 runs up the 1 in 97 gradient past Sheringham Golf Course in September 1993. Photo. Steve Allen

From Sheringham station your train passes under bridge 305, this carries Church Street into the town centre. Shortly, the operating signal box, removed from Wensum Junction at Norwich, is passed on the seaward side, here the signalman hands the driver of your train a 'tablet' which permits him to enter the single line section ahead. Opposite are the original carriage sidings from BR and M&GN days where operational stock not in use is often stored. The train then crosses Sweetbriar Lane automatic level crossing. This is a private road which leads to Sheringham Golf Club. On the seaward side, the golf practice area, followed by the clubhouse and the hilly course of

GWR 2-6-2T No. 4561 at the start of the 1 in 80 climb to Weybourne in April 1996. The woods on Dead Man's Hill are in the background. Photo.Steve Allen

18 holes are seen. Landward, in the distance, you can make out the attractive flint-walled village and church of Upper Sheringham, nestling in the wooded hills. The hills of this area of Norfolk were formed by deposits of morainic materials (sands, gravels, clays, flints) left behind when the ice sheets of the Ice Age melted.

The main coast road (A149) runs alongside the railway for a while, giving motorists the opportunity to stop and wave as they watch the trains go by.

Meanwhile to the north, over the golf course, extensive views of the North Sea appear once the train has passed Skelding Hill with its small white coastguard hut on the top. Here in a natural cleft in the cliffs was located the Old Hythe (Sheringham) Lifeboat House, where a rowing lifeboat was in use until the 1930s, when a motorised one was installed nearer the town.

Your train is now climbing a 1 in 97 gradient. Arable land with typical crops, barley, carrots, sugarbeet, etc., now takes over. The track levels out for a short while before passing under bridge 304 then it descends at 1 in 100 in a cutting through Dead Man's Hill, local legend is that it is called this because the Weybourne victims of the Great Plague were buried here, remote from their homes.

GRADIENT PROFILE OF ROUTE

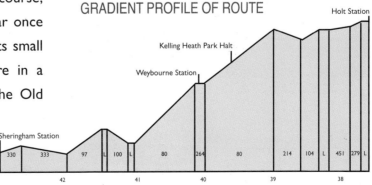

LNER B12 4-6-0 No. 8572 bursts out from under bridge 304 near Weybourne on a footplate experience course in May 1996.
Photo. Steve Allen

Soon the cutting gives way to an embankment which carries the track to bridge 303 over the A149. This bridge was reconstructed almost completely by volunteers in 1984. Sadly, the project leader, experienced bridge-engineer David Pinkerton, lost his life through an accidental fall, when the bridge was almost completed. A plaque to his memory is built into its abutment.

On the landward side you will see woodlands which parallel the line most of the rest of the way to Weybourne station. These form part of the Sheringham Hall estate. Sheringham Hall is a Regency building which is now part of the National Trust and is the work of Humphrey Repton. The grounds are open to the public all year round and in late May and early June there are magnificent displays of rhododendrons which are well worth a visit. Panoramic views of the area, including the railway, are to be seen from the gazebo in the park.

Beyond bridge 303 the engine has to work hard up a gradient of 1 in 80 (yes, in so-called 'flat' Norfolk!), which takes you all the way to Weybourne station. On the seaward side can be seen, first a group of coastguards' cottages close to the cliff edge and then the picturesque windmill which is now a private residence. Weybourne village with its church and priory ruins are soon visible. Just north of the village is Weybourne Hope, where there is very deep water close into the shore making it an ideal point for an invasion of the area, this gave rise to the old rhyme:

"He who would old England win, must at Waborne Hoop begin."

Looking across the fields to Weybourne windmill and the sea. Photo. Steve Allen

Such was the threat that in 1588 it was garrisoned against the Spanish fleet and during the two world wars a large army camp was based here to defend the coast. This camp has closed and is now home to the famous Muckleburgh Military Vehicle Museum. There are also many local tales of smuggling said to have taken place here. On the opposite side, the wooded hills continue with showy rhododendrons in late spring and the golden brown of bracken in autumn.

The line then runs through a short cutting and Weybourne Station is soon reached. If you wish you may break your journey here and continue on a later train. If you are staying on the train it will continue its journey to the end of the line at Holt. At periods of high fire risk it may be necessary for a diesel engine to be put on your train here at Weybourne.

LNER B12 4-6-0 No. 8572 arrives at Weybourne with a train from Sheringham in April 1995. Photo. Steve Allen

WEYBOURNE

Following Clement Scott's Poppyland tourist boom, the M&GN decided that they would attempt to promote Weybourne as a holiday resort. The station with its two platforms was built in 1900 and opened to passengers on 1st July, 1901. The Weybourne Springs Hotel was also built around this time. Due to its late addition to the line Weybourne station is not what we know as a typical M&GN station as it was built in a grand late Victorian style by local craftsmen. The date 1900 is displayed in the brickwork, this being the date that the building was completed.

Your train will arrive on either of the two platforms here, depending on the service operating; note the typical M&GN criss cross trellis fencing. The main station buildings are on the seaward side, access to these from platform one is over the footbridge formerly situated at Stowmarket station on the Norwich to London line. Also on platform one is an operational signal box rescued from Holt in 1967, the original Weybourne box having been demolished by BR

in 1964 along with the waiting room on this platform. The present replica waiting room was built in 1987 by a local Manpower Services scheme.

As you cross the footbridge you get a fine view of the countryside back towards Sheringham and down to the sea, you can watch your train depart from here and if you are waiting for one from Sheringham you will be amazed how far away you can see it as it toils up the gradient. At both ends of the station you can see the unusual M&GN somersault signals, so named because they pivot in the middle rather than at the end. In front of you as you descend the footbridge are the railway's workshops where the engines and carriages are restored and maintained. The operational locomotives are stabled at the Sheringham end of the yard, being prepared here early in the morning for the working day, and disposed at the end of the day. Unfortunately, public access is not normally permitted on Health and Safety grounds, but sometimes guided tours can be arranged, please ask the Stationmaster for details.

The station here has been restored to recreate the late 1930s being painted in the LNER green and cream colour scheme. The former parcels office has been converted into a souvenir shop and buffet to fit the period. The canopied buildings contain a splendid booking hall with a very attractive timbered ceiling, a restored 1930s style booking office, the Society's railway bookshop in the old Stationmaster's office and a porters' room and lamp room. The original ladies waiting room which leads off from the booking hall is now in use as an office.

The station has an attractive setting. To the north, a mile away, lies the village with its church, Augustinian priory ruins and windmill, and beyond these the sea. To the south are the hills and woods of the Cromer Ridge.

If you have time to spare why not take advantage of one of the pleasant nature walks from the station. You can go either through Kelling Woods up on to the top of Kelling Heath or across the fields to Sheringham Park. Both give panoramic views of the surrounding countryside, especially of Weybourne village, windmill and the coast line. There are maps on the station. For Kelling Heath follow the signs westward under bridge 302, and

A friendly driver explains the controls of a locomotive to interested children at Weybourne

for Sheringham Park take the small gate under the footbridge on platform one. In Kelling Woods there is a small platform called Kelling Heath Park Halt. This serves the campsite at the top of the heath. If you wish you may catch a railbus or DMU from here, they stop on request. The steam or diesel hauled trains, however, are only able to stop in the Weybourne direction due to the gradient.

GWR 2-8-0T No. 5224 arrives at Weybourne with a train from Holt in September 1994.
Photo. Steve Allen

Your train continues on from Weybourne, passing under bridge 302, and crossing over Spring Beck at bridge 301. Spring Beck is so named because the stream originates from several springs some twenty yards south of the bridge. The nature trail runs alongside this part of the line before turning into Hundred Acre Wood, now part of Kelling Heath Park. As the train climbs this tough 1 in 80 gradient, fine views of Weybourne village and the sea appear, while opposite was the site of Weybourne Springs Hotel, a large hotel in turreted style, built in the hope that Weybourne would become a popular resort. This was demolished at the start of the second world war as it was thought to be used as a landmark for enemy bombers coming in over the coast.

We soon pass Kelling Heath Park Halt, with its short platform, which serves the large caravan park on Kelling Heath. If you are on a railbus or DMU it may stop here, but steam trains can only stop on the way back to Weybourne from Holt, please let the guard know if you wish to alight here.

Beyond this halt the line continues to climb the lengthy gradient of 1 in 80 through a deep cutting and out on to the open heathland of Kelling Heath, with heather and gorse making splashes of colour at appropriate times of the year. As the train emerges from the cutting it is now at the summit of the line. A privately owned crossing-keeper's cottage stands by an accommodation crossing here which only serves a footpath and bridleway now. This is known as Windmill Crossing as in the past a wind-pump was used to supply water for the cottage.

Carrying on towards Holt, coniferous woodland of the Forestry Commission is passed, and to the seaward side of the line can be seen the gravel pits from which track ballast was extracted for use on the M&GN. The train now passes under Bridge Road bridge 299. The remainder of the journey to the terminus at Holt is through mixed woodland and open countryside.

As your train pulls in to the platform at Holt you will notice on the other side there is a wide triangle of land, this is where the original line of the M&GN was planned to curve round towards Salthouse, Cley and Blakeney. This was never built as the railway company decided that they would be better off continuing on to Cromer instead. There were several later plans to build a branch to Blakeney, all of which failed, but had it been built the junction would have been here.

Hunslet Austerity 0-6-0ST No. 3809 completes the picture for one of the finest views between Weybourne and Holt. Photo. Debbie Allen

HOLT

The platform at Holt was built by volunteers in 1988, and an M&GN style waiting shelter was added in 1992. This is not the site of the original station, which was a mile further along the line towards Melton Constable, now obliterated by Holt's bypass. The line used to pass beneath the old Holt to Cromer road at this spot, and consequently was in a cutting, the bridge was an accident black spot and was removed in the mid-sixties. The cutting had to be filled in and levelled before any track could be laid. From the Sheringham end of the platform you can see across the tracks a former M&GN lampman's hut which has been adapted to be a small signal cabin. Beyond the platform you can see Kelling Hospital, and on the other side of the railway site is the famous Greshams public school.

Your train will stop here for about ten minutes while the engine runs around ready for the journey back to Weybourne and Sheringham, if you wish to alight at Kelling Heath Park Halt please let the guard know before the train leaves so that he can tell the driver to stop there. At present there are few visitor facilities available here at Holt. A temporary building serves as the small but friendly ticket office and souvenir shop. Holt town centre is about a mile away from the station. At peak times there is a privately run horse-drawn bus service which connects with our trains from here to the town centre, which is well worth a visit, being a largely unspoilt Georgian town.

LNER N7 0-6-2T No. 69621 rounds Bridge Road curve near bridge 299 at Holt in September 1995. The M&GN's ballast pits were located on the left hand side of the line here and can now be explored as part of Kelling Heath Park. Photo: Steve Allen

Journey's end - Hunslet Austerity
0-6-0ST No. 3809 runs around its train
at Holt in preparation for the return trip
to Sheringham

SPECIAL EVENTS

The railway holds a number of special events, not only to appeal to the railway enthusiast but also to a wider audience. Steam and diesel gala weekends are staged once or twice a year when the railway puts on an intensive service, including demonstration goods trains. Guest engines are often brought in to provide as much interest as possible. These often stay on the line for a while and supplement the railway's own fleet of locomotives. Themed events are also held, Ladies Days when the men take a backseat and the railway is totally run by female volunteers, and various historical days, when volunteers dress to recreate an era as closely as possible. For the children "Friends of Thomas the Tank Engine" events are held, sometimes with guest visits from Thomas himself! The end of the year culminates in the running of the railway's exceedingly popular Santa Specials where children are taken by train from Sheringham to receive a present from Santa in his magical grotto.

The North Norfolk Railway is also a popular location with TV and film-makers, some of the more well-known programmes and films in which it has appeared include "Dads Army", "Sons and Lovers", "Hi-Di-Hi", "Miss Marple", "Swallows and Amazons", "Waterlands", "Love on a Branch Line", and a Ruth Rendell mystery.

"Thomas" arrives at Weybourne during one of the railway's
"Friends of Thomas the Tank Engine" events
Photo. Steve Allen

Themed weekends are popular on the NNR,
here visiting Manning Wardle 0-6-0ST "Sir Berkeley"
and vintage coach arrive at Sheringham during a "Victorian Weekend".
Photo. Steve Allen

LOOKING TO THE FUTURE

Much has been achieved on the railway since the preservationists took over from British Railways back in 1966. The derelict buildings have been repaired, locomotives and carriages restored to their former glory, the signalling reinstated, and most significantly trains now run through to Holt on track that has been re-laid along the abandoned trackbed from Weybourne.

Even now the volunteers and the railway's small permanent work force are pushing forward with new projects as well as maintaining what has already been achieved. More carriages are under restoration, and locomotives are undergoing major rebuilds. At Weybourne, work has already begun on the erection of a carriage workshop to enable volunteers to restore carriages undercover rather than out at the mercy of the weather. A new station building has yet to be erected at Holt, also at Holt it is intended to build a large museum building to house most of the railway's historic rolling stock. Looking much further into the future, it is hoped to re-erect the missing buildings and canopies at Sheringham that BR demolished in the 1960s.

A question that many visitors ask is whether it is intended to extend the railway any further. The answer is a guarded yes, if possible, the option to go westwards from Holt is no longer possible due to the town's bypass, but should the remaining section of the M&GN line to Cromer become available we would seriously consider the possibility of acquiring it, or seeking running rights from Railtrack, though there would be many obstacles to overcome, both physical and financial, not least the reinstatement of the level crossing in Sheringham.

Finance for the railway projects comes from a number of sources, revenue from running the trains, the sale of shares in the railway, and donations. Projects like the restoration of the B12 and J15 were almost totally funded by donations from members and the public, whereas the extension of the line to Holt was funded by shares and the issue of bearer bonds. If you would like to find out more about becoming a shareholder please ask at Sheringham station or write for a prospectus. Alternatively you could become a member of the railway's supporting society, the Midland and Great Northern Joint Railway Society, benefits of

membership include a quarterly magazine Joint Line providing up-to-date news and photographs of developments on the railway, and reduced rate travel on the North Norfolk Railway.

Volunteers are the life-blood of the railway, without them the whole operation would grind to a halt. New volunteers are always needed to help run the railway, be it driving an engine or digging the gardens, there's a job for someone of almost every age and skill. Even if you can only help once in a while you will be very welcome. If you are interested, please contact the Volunteer Liaison Officer at Sheringham station and he will be only too pleased to find you a suitable opening and make the necessary introductions.

THE EAST COAST PULLMAN

One of the North Norfolk Railway's most successful developments has been the introduction of the East Coast Pullman dining train. The train consists of two splendidly restored 1930s Pullman Cars which once ran as part of the Southern Railway's famous Brighton Belle service, together with a purpose built kitchen car and converted generator coach.

The East Coast Pullman runs on selected Friday and Saturday evenings from Easter to December. Dinner is served during a leisurely trip from Sheringham to Holt and back. Alternatively the train is used on Sundays to serve Roast Sunday lunches. By travelling on these trains, diners can relive the atmosphere of Pullman luxury. All of these services are exceedingly popular, therefore prior booking is essential.

The train is also available for private hire, and can be used for wedding receptions, anniversaries, or for business groups, etc. If you would like details of the East Coast Pullman or any of the railway's other catering services please contact Sheringham station for a brochure.

Pullman Car number 91 at Weybourne.
Photo. Steve Allen

The Romance of
The Railway